MW00582155

EMERGENCES
AND
SPINNER FALLS

New Issues Poetry & Prose

Editor	Herbert Scott
Associate Editor	David Dodd Lee
Advisory Editors	Nancy Eimers, Mark Halliday, William Olsen, J. Allyn Rosser
Assistants to the Editor	Rebecca Beech, Lynnea Page, Derek Pollard, Jonathan Pugh, Marianne E. Swierenga
Assistant Editors	Kirsten Hemmy, Erik Lesniewski, Adela Najarro, Margaret von Steinen
Editorial Assistant	Jennifer Abbott
Business Manager	Michele McLaughlin
Fiscal Officer	Marilyn Rowe

New Issues Poetry & Prose
The College of Arts and Sciences
Western Michigan University
Kalamazoo, MI 49008

An Inland Seas Poetry Book

 Inland Seas poetry books are supported by a grant from
The Michigan Council for Arts and Cultural Affairs.

First Edition, 2002.

ISBN   1-930974-20-5 (paperbound)

Library of Congress Cataloging-in-Publication Data:
Haight, Robert
Emergences and Spinner Falls/Robert Haight
Library of Congress Control Number: 2002104231

Art Direction	Joseph Wingard
Design	Jun Ku Kang
Production	Paul Sizer
	The Design Center, Department of Art
	College of Fine Arts
	Western Michigan University

EMERGENCES
AND
SPINNER FALLS

ROBERT HAIGHT

New Issues

WESTERN MICHIGAN UNIVERSITY

for Gary Steinecker and Patti Haight Steinecker
and for Tomasa, always

This dewdrop world
Is a dewdrop world
And yet . . .
　　　　　—Issa

Contents

Acknowledgments

Thanks to the editors of the following publications in which versions of these poems first appeared:

The Bridge: "Water Music"

Controlled Burn: "Fish Flies," "Early Steelhead in a Late Year"

The Driftwood Review: "When You Have Lived with a River," "How Is It That the Snow"

Joyride: "Two Dogs with Children"

The Kalamazoo Gazette: "Come with Me"

Northeast: "This River," "Nymphs"

Passages North: "Learning to Fly"

South Coast Poetry Journal: "The Desire to Farm," "Baloney"

Wayne Review: "The Month of Rain"

"Issa Casts a Dry Fly at the Moon," "This River," "Two Dogs with Children," and "Fish Flies" appeared in *New Poems From the Third Coast*, Wayne State University Press.

"The Hand That Is a Fin" appeared in *Contemporary Michigan Poetry*, Wayne State University Press.

Some of these poems appeared in the chapbook *Water Music*, published by Ridgeway Press.

Thanks to the Arts Foundation of Michigan for its support.

I

This River

This is the river
that didn't appear on the map

that spread across the end
of one of those endless two-tracks
angling off a logging road

or, perhaps, it wasn't a two-track
at all, just a space between the trees
that you mistook and ended here.

No tracks but the curve
of deer hooves in the bank sand,
the path of ancients
disappearing into brush.

The river surges by,
its unmistakable clarity.
Even in the pines
on the far bank, each needle
sparks a single fire
rubbed from it by the wind.

Nymphs

The river keeps its secrets.
Under the swollen hide
of submerged logs, in the deadfalls,
a pulse beats as slowly as in a coma.

You might have seen the woman dance
wearing a string of pearls,
spinning until the pearls and beads of sweat
sprinkled light over all the dry grass
of a hundred dumb faces

or wearing deer hide and leather boots
kicking the top of a barroom table,
whirling in a fog of cigarette smoke.
You might have seen her become
a swirling butterfly.

When spring sheds its skin
under the jams and in the lap
of granite, these small transformations:
the stoneflies wobbling out onto the banks
like sailors on first leave,

mayflies sloughing off
their casing, knifing to the surface,
the wing-drumming blur
of a new hatch.

Each of us falls into the river.
We feel it pour like fear through our hair.
Then we get up,
chilled, dripping and changed.

8

Reading the Water

It's enough to know where you are
when the river narrows and spreads,
coils and stretches into an evening
that sprinkles scotch into the green shadows
of reeds and trees.

There is a turn that tunnels into dark all day
where an oak pendulum rows
a long rhythmic sentence,
and there are straits flecked with boulders,
a constellation of moons
holding their faces to the light.

Even if you don't know where you are
you follow water that knows its course,
whether you wriggle awake from a nightmare
or stare into the thin mortality of the mirror.

In the dark pocket under the boulder,
behind the long fingers of ripples
reaching from nests of branches,
an old trout keeps time,
evening slides down the trunks
and memory is a wavering shape
in the weeds and long strands of grass.

The air buzzes and spits specks of fire.
The river pulls every possibility downstream.

On Dowagiac Creek

When shadows pour from the corners
of pools, extending like fog from brush
and overhanging branches,
white mayflies appear along the corridor
of the creek where the last glimpse of light
holds the water,

the way a few flakes of snow,
descending, multiply,
soon filling the air, veering and gusting
their illumination of the wind's geometry.

I wade slowly back downstream
remembering December walks in the snow,
when porch lights looked like faraway lighthouses
and snow speckled a tunnel of darkness.

The mayflies melt on the water.
The cloud spinning above the surface
gives just enough light to find my way
back to the bridge—and summer.

Early Steelhead in a Late Year

Staring into water, we see our own drowned faces
but we drift up and downstream
through dawn fog that presses against the empty

space above the water, casting not on faith
so much as what we remember: melted muck trail
winding the bank, air scented with ground thaw.

There are no visible signs of them,
no constellations of stone buffed into redds
or surges of silver light knifing the pools

though we are sure they will return.
We will fish into the night,
waiting for the flex of a rod,

the explosion of water
when the fishing gets as easy
as it must have been for the Twelve,

who saw Lazarus emerge from the grave
dripping with new life,
or those who witnessed Christ
walk across the surface of the sea.

Issa Casts a Dry Fly at the Moon

A white stone in moonlight
as black curls of water
shadow its edges
and pass downstream
into the further darknesses
under the pine trees

he wears a purple gown
the color of night sky
and casts a strand of spider web
at the moon
floating on the river

for a trout
whose skin is empty space
and whose scales are stars
to take this fly
he has spun from the thin air
of his breath

so he can see the moon shatter
and watch the river's hands
ease the pieces together
into one moon again

as if there were no trout
hiding under the moon
whispering *current, current, current*

II

Thelonius in Michigan

A few days in January
sunlight pierces the darkness
like a clever thought.
The headlights lose their tentacles.
From the branches and wires,
from slim fingers of ice,
the beads begin to fall,
rosaries in unexpected cadences.
This is all Michigan has to offer
in January, when sparrows
cloud the gray sky every day,
but this winter that will not love you
holds you more than one that is too easy,
yet will not let go.

Do the smokestacks
exhale fresh air scented with sandalwood?
Or do rainbows light again
the silver skin of the trout?
Has that woman
alone so many years opened the door
to the delighted shrieks of children,
who wanted only to bury their faces
in the pure folds of her apron?

The vane spins on its axis.
Tonight, sleet will undercoat a blizzard.
The hot air grates smell like locker rooms.
But a south wind brushes our faces,
combs the puddles on the pavement.
We hear old bones in the lurching trees.
And a day when the sun pours over everything
in January, in Michigan, we celebrate
nothing for all the right reasons.

Winter Showers

There is first
the hiss of maracas
and the body
unfolding itself
to the sultry
Brazilian air,
slowly undulating
to a samba
played note by note
with a light touch
to the skin,
the entire length
of the body
immersed in a cocoon
of steam.
You can stay here forever,
the air whispers,
tossing its hair,
yet
business in the north
pulls you,
its gravity
a motion
that makes your body gag,
and you wince,
knowing that death
rises through the soles
when you take that step
on the cold tile floor.

The Month of Rain

In the month of rain
trees turned to sponge eclipse the sun's thin shadow.
A leaf range clots sewers along the curb
and the wind, nothing more than a downdraft,
bends tall grass. The suburbs block in storm
windows and squirrels come down to gather
all they own.
          Take a walk in the month of rain
and you'll end up in that part of town
where alleys wear black leather and streets turn
on each other.
          But lovers do not pull
from one another toward the world. Their bodies
become tributaries to the one direction water knows,
the branches merge to one stream,
silence at the river mouth.

We accept this clouded beauty. In the month of rain
we throw up our hands, we let go.

The Desire to Farm

She reaches among the marigolds
and petunias that fill a small bed
in the front yard, clawing at the dirt
on hands and knees. Behind her, the fields
unroll into sky. The barn drips
shadows onto the pigweed. She works
a square piece of ground cut out of the lawn
near a sprawling elm and for a moment
you consider her figure balanced
on its shape, how you would walk
into this life that smells of freshly cut grass.
In the house, the towels will be folded
and stacked. Bread will rise under its pure
aroma in the kitchen. You would give
up your name and all that you have built
of yourself to become as facile
and anonymous as field grass,
as this woman whose skin is as simple
as earth. You turn the car slowly
into the dirt drive and she looks up
at you, smiling. You decide to live
out your life with her, leaving your
briefcase to rot in the back seat.
You will dig out the mailbox
and throw it into the ravine
where each year it will rust until so thin
and brown it dissolves, the way the landscape
in the rearview mirror disappears
from the dust of your tires
as you head down the highway.

Water Music

The music does not cost him
as it rides out on the wind
and sails across the water.
He has anchored his boat
where weeds curl among themselves,
fifty yards off the shore, and sits
with a six-pack of Harp,
a styrofoam cup of loam and crawlers
and his pole, resting on an oarlock.
Tonight he fishes to Haydn,
next Saturday, Vivaldi.
He has checked the program.
What does not change is the sun,
orange and swollen in the trees
that bank the lake, the nervous cloud
of a new hatch, the rhythm of water.
He catches rock bass and bluegill
that rattle the surface like cymbals.
This does not fold into music
but rises distant from it,
nearer him, and adds to its beauty
the way a certain light or the leaves
of bushes make a person beautiful
by their surrounding,
as he appears in his boat
a shadow grown from shadow
poised on a shimmer,
when the audience looks beyond itself,
beyond the musicians and stands,
following a strand of music
into the open evening air.

Pinecone

This could be
the work of a whittler
who sat with a knife
on a front porch
that looked forever
into the sunset
over a pine tree

or a rose, petrified
by a millennium
of spring rains

Learning to Fly

The first desire of the child
is to fly, which is why children
after crawling or standing,
walking or finally learning to run
are often found perched
atop a stack of books on a high chair,
hanging, one hand on the wall,
the other clutching a light fixture,
peering up, up, as if the earth
were another womb to break free from,

and once we resign ourselves to life
on foot, it becomes the desire of dreams,
so the dream becomes possibility,
and waking, a kind of disappointment.
We try to fall back to sleep
before the dream flies away
but arrive in time to feel only the brush
of wind from its feathers

until finally,
a life of this desire takes form
and in old age
we come to resemble birds,
hands stiffened to claws,
eyes darting around our heads
which seem to tilt back
as if setting a course,
as if we will grow wings
sometime very soon.

First Day of Fall

The sun hovers behind a cataract
and the day rises in mist,
the grass and trees grown
deeply into their shadows.
Wind exhales a cold steam
over the sweating leaves,
over the lake's dim vacancies,
and when I press my arms
around the bulk of my sweater
and look out into the lake,
the chill carves my features,
the skin lightening as if holiness
were a matter of degree.
Some days you can't tell
whether you've opened your eyes.
The bleached dock
slumps in the lapping waves,
tearing away plank by plank
like the pages of a calendar.
I spend this day
gathering the scattered tusks
of driftwood into piles.
Tonight, the cabin will glow.
From the hearth, a fire of shadows.

Apples

This year we drove to a farm
to buy apples for pies and cider, bread and sauce,
apples stuffed with sauerkraut,
stuffed with sausage and baked, sautéed with bacon.
This would require pounds of red and golden delicious,
gravenstein and yellow transparent, wealthy,
grimes golden, jonathon, macintosh—early
and late—courtland, york imperial, rhode island greening,
newtown pippin, baldwin, rome beauty,
nothern spy, stayman and winesap.
So we raced from the city that golden autumn afternoon
to load apple crates into the trunk
to cart home our slice of the orchard.
A sign in the front yard read
Centennial Farm. This farm has been in one family
for over a hundred years, and it cheered us
to know these people must have grown
from a history of apples.
We walked across a dirt drive to the barn,
dust clouding our ankles,
where a woman talked to a man—apple talk—
and the bins overflowed a rainbow of apples
and apple must hung in the air.
We waited until we ran out of bins
and bushels to pretend to inspect,
yet no proposal for sale had been tendered,
and the dark barn shadowed the blush
that had risen to our cheeks on the drive
and we withdrew and kicked at straw.
A couple of kids tore around like dogs
pulling each other ragged and then ran off.
Our son and daughter inspected barnwood;
I wasn't sure what a halfpeck was,

and when the farmer, whose narrow head stuck out
from his beard, finally labored over and drawled
about what he could get me, I foundered
and pointed toward a pile.
His woman, or sister, lurched off to get cider
(a gallon for half the price you'd pay in a store),
and I threw a bunch of apples into a grocery bag
and started my wife and kids toward the car,
where we would either meet the woman again
or one of those pedigreed children
as we drove out and grabbed
the cider, because
all they did was talk (and not much of that,
either) about the weeks and weeks it takes
for apples to grow sweeter,
and I just couldn't stand it any longer; I mean,
I just didn't have the stomach for that.

Autumnal

In a time of milkchutes and clear bottles
autumn ripens on the limbs
and leaf smoke spirals up the drives,
brushing the sky's lucid enamel.

Somehow, through all the washings,
a scent of humus lingers in sweatshirts,
though the names of the colleges have long since
fractured into crumbled marble.
Summer's gold skin lightens under wool
and the vegetable man becomes possible again.

October is never quite here.
Years rattle its flannel leaves,
a paramnesia of gourds and Indian corn
strung on porches, like a face
grinning in the window
before we recognize the reflection.

Now that crisp air hones the edges of the days
and trees sprinkle rust with every gust of wind,
the orchard sags with fruit again
and we return with our old baskets and names.

The Hand That Is a Fin

1
I stand beside my grandmother
and son as they hold hands.
Hers petrified in a slow arc
from flesh to stone.
His, on their slender stems,
still wet behind the buds.

2
This nursing home hangs no paintings.
My father stares into them,
day and night, three floors above us.
He does not hear my son's voice,
rising small shouts in Grandma's room,
but she can hear now.
She clasps his wrist like dirt.
When his hand opens
there is a crease in it
I hadn't noticed before,
a red line
ninety years long.

3
At Bear Creek
salmon fan their eggs as if rocking them.
Later, they move below their beds
into the shadow of a log or boulder
and wait to die.
          One fall,
day after day I came back to watch
a salmon swaying to the same music,
his scales melting before me,
the skin darkening slowly.

4
Now he is shadow.
The only fight left is his bulk.
The stones of his bed
sparkle around him.
Soon the shadow will split with light,
waterweeds will sprout between mossy stones,
the shadow and stone will blend into green.

5
The hand that is a rock erodes.
The hand that is a blossom wilts,
its petals blowing across backyards and fields.
But the hand that is a fin
strums a slow guitar.
A man stands in shadow, listening,
for that moment neither father nor son.

III

Two Dogs with Children

Say you've just come over the hump
and can see one dog on the side of the highway,
ribbons of blood and drool flagging
from its mouth, trickling
off the shoulder into rust-stained dirt.
It is the dog that has chased your car
each morning on your way to work,
made you brake as it trotted
ahead of your left front tire,
until far enough from home it turned
away and you could accelerate to sixty-five.
Four kids stand around
where their front yard meets the road.
It is their dog but they haven't moved it.
They are waiting for someone to get home.
You crawl past them, see their eyes turn
to where their dog fixes
its stare into a tiny galaxy of asphalt,
while their other dog keeps its distance,
its long coat slapped to life
from a stream of wind by the barn.
None of it helps.
The next Monday they wait
for the school bus and watch
the other dog become the first,
tearing after every truck and car cruising by,
snarling at the bus tires.
Each morning you pass
the dog is still alive,
crouched to jump in front of your car
while the children look down, embarrassed,
perhaps as much for their bright nylon coats
and rubber boots, or the junk busses

and rusted sixties pickups
rotting in the weeds that make up their yard,
as for any training they owe their dog.
And so I ask what do you do?
Do you stop and shout at them
to get that goddamn dog off the road,
to tie it to a chain and when it starts
after the wheels to yank it back until it learns?
Or do you roll down the window
and touch their hair,
one dog already crushed
before their eyes?
Or do you just drive ahead,
let leash laws and agencies promise
all the necessary repairs?

Baloney

I lied at my first confession, after going blank
on sins. I had studied the opening, the wood slat
sliding up like a cocked guillotine, my two lines
that started it all. When the priest asked what I had
committed, I froze, then blurted out that I ate
meat on Friday, that I opened the refrigerator,
saw a piece of meat and ate it. He asked what kind
of meat: a leftover steak maybe or a chicken leg?
I told him a piece of baloney and that I shoved it
down bare, without dressing it with lettuce or bread.
He asked if I had to confess anything else; I said
just that I lied. Then he whispered in Latin, and didn't
stop though a growl welled up from his stomach
that sounded like the Beast himself. Five Our Fathers
and ten Hail Marys later, I got home for lunch.
The next year they removed the sin from Friday meat.
I thought there was something divine in that too:
the mystery of my faith, the host held aloft, that white,
perfect circle the exact fit for a slice of baloney.

Fish Flies

Fish flies filled that June night, drawn from the lake to the lights along shore, clouds boiling in the halo of every street light. Fish flies covered each brick on the houses, curtained the windows of the storefronts, coated the screens. We were sixteen, driving around in the glow of dashlights behind a cloud of smoke we passed from hand to hand. We circled the courts back to Lakeshore Road, the odometer spinning miles out of nothing but some urgency to glimpse the bodies of the girls we desired, silhouetted by translucent wings on the twitching panes of their bedroom window. We listened to the low drone of a Seger tape, the fish flies crackling like static under the tires. In the morning the shopkeepers would sweep piles off the sidewalks with a push broom. We would hear of a few cars that slid out of control where fish flies had packed into a thin layer like ice. We didn't know they survived for years in the shallow mud until the night they shed their skins and flew in search of a mate. We thought they only lived for one day, pulled the smell of lake water over the night, over us, and left it there.

On a Still Summer Afternoon

The heron
posing on the stump offshore
considers the dimensions of fish

while
the largemouth bass
peeking through water lilies
measures
the height of his jump

both waiting
waiting
not a ripple
on the water

A Walk at Sunrise

What begins this day
is an orange halo rising into the violet sky,
and the lake, a dim movement of the night.
Dawn mist hangs like old clothes
where the heron tucks its head into its sleeve.
I walk along the edge of Hemlock Lake,
inhaling the dank breeze,
an animation of the early rising morning.
The headstones of dew
evaporate from each grass blade
as sunshine fells them row after row.
I am pulled along by light.
Now my skin is porous.
The wind rubs itself against my arms.

Sunrise on 96th Avenue East

Sometimes light falls
in columns toward the ground,

in streams through thick, dank morning air,
and fires each leaf and blade of grass,

everything green. Mornings like this,
one might believe heaven could be

just above the clouds. In a moment
of grace as ordinary as any morning,

the mind opens again to this soft rain
of light.

Come with Me

Come with me into November.
The fields are amber stubble:
dried husks, tufts of straw
and weeds turned to bone.

In October, a rotting pumpkin
rose instead of the moon.
We celebrated the Dead Festivals
and dressed in spirit rags.

Now darkness floods the lowlands
of morning, pours over the ledge of dusk.

Though deer slip from the thicket
searching a scant green memory of summer,
some flowering after the bitter frost,
this is the time of their mating.
Don't stand at the window watching for snow.

How Is It That the Snow

How is it that the snow
amplifies the silence,
slathers the black bark on limbs,
heaps along the brush rows?

Some deer have stood on their hind legs
to pull the berries down.
Now they are ghosts along the path,
snow flecked with red wine stains.

This silence in the timbers.
A woodpecker on one of the trees
taps out its story,
stopping now and then in the lapse
of one white moment into another.

IV

When You Have Lived with a River

for Galway Kinnell

I

When you have lived with a river
the first curve below the falls
reminds you of the boulder
shedding iron light under the surface
or a sunken log, covered with algae,
nodding in the current six steps downstream,
or how the riffle begins in the straightaway
where the shallows glisten
as the current washes over the calls of robins and jays,
shrieks of crows, rising above the water
into a river of wind on which a heron glides.
          Leaves of the last autumn,
spines of branch tumbling,
careening off the edges of stones,
the wing-cased nymphs that taxi
toward flight, grains of sand glowing amber
as they extract a glint of sunlight, globes
of oxygen pulled toward the big water
that quiets as it stretches into six directions
and becomes blue as sky, indistinguishable from sky,
the single universe of space
when you have lived with a river.

II

When you have lived with a river
you stand in its embrace, feeling the river move
around you and pull through the pilings
of your legs, then downstream,
flowing over the great oak that ten years before
began to show the web of roots where the bank edged back.
One day it tottered in the wind,
its weight against the open air
fell into the hands of gravity,
and it collapsed across the banks.
            A year later, the deadfall shapes
the flow: a hundred yards of shallow stone fan out
from the fallen trunk. Above the trunk a hole,
black as space.
You watch the river change, the way a tree grows rings,
feel the shallow imprint of your boots,
the distinct and permanent conception of yourself
making a sound so slight no tree can hear it
when you have lived with a river.

III

When you have lived with a river
you drift along the body of a snake
past sheer banks of pine and hemlock,
where the river disappears as the slopes subside
into the shadow tunnel of limbs,
aspen and maples reaching across the water
that grow into a meshed ceiling of leaves
                and the river streaming
over slabs of granite,
in recesses of the undercut shore,
the wind lifting the boughs and rattling leaves
as the heron streams like a shooting star, veering
mirror of the river's flow, the river etched
into the heron as a trail burned out of the trees,
and you, below the wind, as much the river
in the heron's eyes as any log or stone.

IV

When you have lived with a river
you see what time shapes out of persistence:
rivulet from stone, stair-step rapids
through the gorge, boulder-littered wash cascading
into the sand pools.
        Ontonagan, Dowagiac,
Laughing Whitefish, the Bear snoring under the hummock.
Cold purity of water, necklace of bone dangling from a cloud,
the mountain walking into the bay.
        Downstream, St. Joseph, Pere Marquette,
mud banks below the dam lined with mansions
on a canal dredged from Eden to Apocalypse.
River of black ink, river of paint, river of fire
endless as the horizon, slow, slow water,
the fish gasping for myths to breathe.

V

When you have lived with a river
the river means nothing beyond itself.
It is not the river of your youth
that you ached for when you desired perfection,
nor the river of the old man or woman
deepened into a silent pool.
All the jewels you wore were another river,
the roads, streets and highways you traveled
to make your face appear in the mirror
were another river,
the veins and arteries streaming blue and red water,
the capillaries stretching across the desert of your eyes,
the presences of those you loved that visited you
in the darkness were another river,
the lines of all the pages you ever read,
the lightning that split the midnight sky, the dreams,
the evenings you watched the sun drown in the lake
were another river.

VI

When you have lived with a river
you begin to understand the language of water,
when shelf ice cracks and bursts into clouds,
the torrent after March rains
as hoarfrost opens its fist from the spongy ground,
the infant giggle of low August
when the rocky, log-strewn bottom
lies naked under the moonlight.
You know the river fills with red, gold, green, brown
leaves swept down on the last warm days of October,
Indian Summer, when salmon surge against the flow
to enact birth from their decay,
buffing the redds until the stones glisten like constellations,
the salmon fading to black in the middle of the stars
as if its body were a long day turning toward dusk,
the dorsal waving a flag in the breeze
as fins ice over with fungal snow
and the beginning and end pass one another in the current,
the balm of water over tattered scales,
the many fingers of water, the single hum of current
when you have lived with a river.

VII

When you have lived with a river
you have seen the stars tremble on the water
as dusk rises from the dew-soaked ground,
their fire more luminous as night settles
into the trees and brush draped in fog along the bank
and finally over the river itself
as you press against the clear pane of its surface
        and then let go, speeding through space,
speeding through heaven and the stars,
the constellations like moonlit stones
and the gravel touched by moonlight
scattering stardust across the deepening sky,
the slick oil of the pool, eddy spinning light
until the salmon tail of a breeze
sweeps the galaxy downstream
and the heron of calm chasing the breeze,
the universe born anew
when you have lived with a river.

photo by Lynne Morrison

Robert Haight was born in Detroit and educated at Michigan
State University and Western Michigan University. His articles,
essays, and poems have appeared in *The Rockford Review*,
Oxford Magazine, *The South Coast Poetry Journal*, *South Florida
Poetry Review*, *Louisville Review*, *The Passages North Anthology*,
Contemporary Michigan Poetry, *New Poems From the Third Coast*,
and elsewhere. He has won awards from the Poetry Resource
Center of Michigan, Western Michigan University, the
Kalamazoo Foundation, and the Arts Foundation of Michigan.
An avid fly fisherman and committed environmentalist, he
teaches writing at Kalamazoo Valley Community College and
lives at Hemlock Lake in Cass County, Michigan.

New Issues Poetry & Prose

Editor, Herbert Scott

Vito Aiuto, *Self-Portrait as Jerry Quarry*

James Armstrong, *Monument In A Summer Hat*

Michael Burkard, *Pennsylvania Collection Agency*

Anthony Butts, *Fifth Season*

Kevin Cantwell, *Something Black in the Green Part of Your Eye*

Gladys Cardiff, *A Bare Unpainted Table*

Kevin Clark, *In the Evening of No Warning*

Jim Daniels, *Night with Drive-By Shooting Stars*

Joseph Featherstone, *Brace's Cove*

Lisa Fishman, *The Deep Heart's Core Is a Suitcase*

Robert Grunst, *The Smallest Bird in North America*

Robert Haight, *Emergences and Spinner Falls*

Mark Halperin, *Time as Distance*

Myronn Hardy, *Approaching the Center*

Edward Haworth Hoeppner, *Rain Through High Windows*

Cynthia Hogue, *Flux*

Janet Kauffman, *Rot* (fiction)

Josie Kearns, *New Numbers*

Maurice Kilwein Guevara, *Autobiography of So-and-so: Poems in Prose*

Ruth Ellen Kocher, *When the Moon Knows You're Wandering*

Steve Langan, *Freezing*

Lance Larsen, *Erasable Walls*

David Dodd Lee, *Downsides of Fish Culture*

Deanne Lundin, *The Ginseng Hunter's Notebook*

Joy Manesiotis, *They Sing to Her Bones*

Sarah Mangold, *Household Mechanics*

David Marlatt, *A Hog Slaughtering Woman*

Gretchen Mattox, *Goodnight Architecture*

Paula McLain, *Less of Her*

Sarah Messer, *Bandit Letters*

Malena Mörling, *Ocean Avenue*

Julie Moulds, *The Woman with a Cubed Head*

Marsha de la O, *Black Hope*

C. Mikal Oness, *Water Becomes Bone*
Elizabeth Powell, *The Republic of Self*
Margaret Rabb, *Granite Dives*
Rebecca Reynolds, *Daughter of the Hangnail; The Bovine Two-Step*
Martha Rhodes, *Perfect Disappearance*
Beth Roberts, *Brief Moral History in Blue*
John Rybicki, *Traveling at High Speeds*
Mary Ann Samyn, *Inside the Yellow Dress*
Mark Scott, *Tactile Values*
Martha Serpas, *Côte Blanche*
Diane Seuss-Brakeman, *It Blows You Hollow*
Marc Sheehan, *Greatest Hits*
Sarah Jane Smith, *No Thanks—and Other Stories* (fiction)
Phillip Sterling, *Mutual Shores*
Angela Sorby, *Distance Learning*
Russell Thorburn, *Approximate Desire*
Rodney Torreson, *A Breathable Light*
Robert VanderMolen, *Breath*
Martin Walls, *Small Human Detail in Care of National Trust*
Patricia Jabbeh Wesley, *Before the Palm Could Bloom: Poems of Africa*